D1590234

SCARS

By Amy Madden Taylor

Cover painting *Hold* by Lara Viana,
Oil on board, 2008
40 x 35 cm.
Courtesy Domo Baal Gallery
Artwork photo by Andy Keate

Cover design: Bo Schager at Belpid.se

CONTENTS

COUNTING

When my sister taught me about sex
we were sitting on the Step of Blood.

First step was the Baby Step
where the little ones sat
while we played hopscotch
on the lower walk
because someone in 1902
had the foresight to pave in
five perfect flat rectangles for
endless chalking, hopping,
and jumping the one-eighty with precision.

Our coveted bits of slate
were pitched exclusively
from the Potsy Step,
the second.

Third was the Wishing Step
where you sat once you were old enough,
because all children know
three is magical.

Fourth was the Step of Blood
where I gashed my knee and had stitches
and you could still see the stain,
also where we exchanged things female.

Fifth was the Step of Confession,
for when you had a secret
because no one on the hopscotch
board would hear.

Sixth was the Emerald City.

The seventh you had to skip
and the eighth—
well, you were already on the flagstone
so it didn't count.

Kids on our block remembered
which step they were on

when they heard things
when they saw things.
We logged the daily coming and going
of visitors and our fathers.
These were always a multiple of two--
I figured that out--
except when ours never called
to say he moved out,
or the time Johnny B's dad
had his fatal heart attack at work.
We were in the Emerald City that night
with a pack of Marlboros
learning how to inhale.

I was on the seventh step
reading about Amelia Earhart
when Matt Levitt touched my Vee
and asked me what it was.
I said it is called FUCKYOU like your face
and he kicked me.
Later my brother Luke came
with his highest level sword
which was a white picket
from the garbage-can fence
and gave Matt a scar.
After that all girls skipped the Seventh Step.

LUCIFER

No one calls her brother Lucifer
but I do.
Long tall Lucifer
with the sunburn and the lies
and the sexy teen vogue model dreams
is sleeping
with mounds of small stuffed animals
like a boy with a soft heart.

Nearest moon in eighteen years
spotlights odd shore-junk
washed up by high tide
and left naked by low--
things that float, or used to--
some you want to take with you,
some you don't dare touch.

Luna-sea: my mad undertow,
burden of a verb for a surname
as though Ellis Island scribes
thought on the ferry there and back
about parts of speech
or even looked up
or knew about moonlight,
or could tell
a nervous gull cry
from the babies' choir.

Shine on---
someone's memory is singing,
even though it won't.
The Man is a myth
and the light is a mirror;
something like this--
or the face is a rabbit
and life is butter dream.

BALTIMORE

My sister Jean Marie
ate flower seeds
said it would make us beautiful.
I swallowed seven packs with
a bottle of orange crush for luck.

When Johnnie B left the pile of comic books—
all Superman and Archie, my best--
I knew it was the zinnias but
sent away for pansies this time--
asters, morning glories--
anything but daffodils which make your
nose grow long, according to my sister.

Pale girls like Jean Marie
are filled with light,
born in the dawn, soft cry of young lambs
pink ears ringing with the song of loons
recipe calling for cups and cups
of moonjuice.

Dark girls like me
are made of soil and earth
and stay awake at night to listen,
remember how our mother wept at birth.
But we are Faithful, we are strong
and when we die for you
it takes much longer for the bones
to turn to dust.

If you starve your skin grows papery thin
until the light comes through.
Eyes are the holes in the map of your face,
veins show green and blue
like roads and rivers
but pupils get jet-blacker.

Today my name is Baltimore.
When you cry your skin runs down
and when it dries your face is paper-old.
You need to hide behind your hair.
Tears of dark-haired girls are acid rain;
Jean Marie's are salty pearls and rare.

4

HOPE (SCARS)

Mama is writing poems
and me, except the hair, I have her gifts,
Jean-Marie says,
although I'd rather the hair.
I find them under the bed—crumpled handwriting
with the dustclusters and sweater-chest,
the warm smell of mothballs
that Lucifer says can get you high
but leaves me dizzy.
When I swallow it feels wrong.
Schoolfood makes me choke;
my bones are nearly small as Jane's.
Today Tillary's Mom said I am thin
enough to be a
model, like Lucifer's Invisible Man kit--
colored plastic held together with clear glue
that gets him high. This can't be right.
A magazine girl, Jean Marie explains.
She saves me her desserts;
says she can see through my face. No matter how much
rice pudding I eat
I'll never be as soft and lovely
as my Jeanie M.
Eat, Hope, and I'll let you wear my ring,
she says.

I am only hungry for words,
things I put into my notebook pages,
maybe for DC to touch me just
the way he did last night.
I can feel it like a scar on my left cheek.
I borrowed the dissecting knife again;
it felt warm in my coat pocket.
I have so many scars now,
even though no one can see.
Soon that will be all that's left of me—
the notebook, scars,
and maybe some graffiti
like the lines I left in the bathroom stall
at Nightingale's diner with DC
where today after vanilla milkshakes
I made a very small mark in my arm…
something about Keats.

5

BABY JANE

Namby Pamby Huckery Suckery
When you summer daysleep
Hoverbees come to tease.

Strawberry mawberry bumble buzz pie
Fly around the fly until the naproom air
is hot and diapery
so they can sting you when you climb
out of your crib.
Your mother says it was a dream
the bees are in your eyes
It isn't true you cannot say
but you can only shake and shake your head
No more naps.

Summer is hot and itchy.
You keep waiting for the snow
to make it better
but screens are on the door
to let the summer in
and ice is melting in Mama's drinkglass.
First they drip tears then it runs away.
I am looking finding where the ice hides…
crawling through the feet to find
someplace in the treetops
where they will not lift me.

I can ride a bird but most fly fast
before I can hold them,
dance on the sill in the morning,
sing a teasing song about my bear.
They want him to come and play
but he is a sleeping bear.
They will carry him to the ice trees
so I must hold him tight
because beaks are prickity
and bears get shivery.

Sun is a fire that burns your eyelids
if you look at it *no no NO*…
The eye of the stove will burn your hand.
Open the oven mouth.

Cookies are melting inside.
Sisters are coloring,
crayons don't stay in your hand.
They roll,
taste cool and blue-violet pointy
like candles.
No no they say don't touch
but you can put your finger through the hole
the moon punched in the black sky.

In the mirror is a baby just like you
but cool
and lick-smooth.
See the baby.
You have moon eye-holes.
You *can* see through-- you *can*
taste like a candle.

JOHNNY B's BROTHER

Johnny B's brother
jumped off the garage roof
with his sister's old duck-handled
candy-stripe umbrella
fully open and learned about war.
Now he has to wear a cast for 8 weeks.
Lucifer went next to make him feel better
smashed his face in the mud
couldn't breathe for a few minutes
but I think he was faking.
He got punished anyway--
we all did-- for *stupidity*, Mama says,
because even if you are just watching
and you don't tell, you are still
punishable, she said, as she whacked my bottom. *Hiney*,
Velma Washington's Mom calls it and *tuckus*,
old Mr. Goldberg says.

Things people call me:
Skinny-Ass, by Lucifer
a Merry Can, by Juana-Lupe
who cleans the girlsroom at school,
a Gens-Fille, by Mme. Anderson
who teaches French on Fridays,
Cunt by the scary homeless guy
who sleeps
on the corner of Elm and Graham
and gives nightmares.

If I told on Johnny B.'s brother
Johnny B. would call me a tattletale.
His brother wouldn't have that cool cast
and the duck umbrella would still be opening.
He wouldn't have been a hero.
Some heroes are dead heroes, Mama says.
I am thinking about my Papa,
thinking if there is no war
he is probably not dead.
Good as dead, Lucifer says.

LISTS

I keep lists in my notebook,
THINGS I NEED FOR CHRISTMAS,
BOOKS I HAVE READ,
GIRLS WHOSE ROOMS I HAVE SEEN,
BOYS I HAVE KISSED,
EVERY SINGLE THING ABOUT: (DC).

After the blue index tab
THINGS TO CONFESS.
Some of them I only draw.
Some of them I list:
1. I've never been to New Mexico
even though I said I had in Global.
2. I lied when I told DC
I knew what he meant
that first time. I just wanted him
to keep talking.
3. Under BOYS I HAVE KISSED is only
two names.
4. I'm bad at cards.
I don't like throwing things away.
Mama says that's funny.
She says cards are good for people--
they teach you to throw things out.
She says all things are dispensable.
Like Pez, you mean? I asked once.
She thought that was funny, too.

I have other lists called
THINGS I NEVER DREAMED OF.
Under this is DC.
Tillary says it's because I am
consciously thinking about him 24/7
and a dream is sub-conscious.
I have him penciled in just in case.
Waiting. Three semesters and one summer.

TRIPS WE NEVER TOOK:
California.
New Mexico.

THINGS I HAVE TO TOUCH:

9

Icing.
Candlefire.
DC. Not.
Myself. Not.

THINGS THAT MAKE MAMA LAUGH THESE DAYS:
Jane.

PIRATES

You don't go to jail
for being mean to sisters,
for snakes, for stealing marbles,
cutting doll hair,
touching.
But there are laws against
killing a praying mantis.
Was it because it was praying?
You'll be sorry, I said.
How many times sorry I can't say.
I thought it was a cricket,
he said through his teeth
but we knew better.

Pirates on the picnic table boat,
old head-rags stained with
29-cent nail polish.
My job was to paint the wounds.
You're no good with swords, says Lucifer
who leaves out the *w*
and has a black patch over his left eye
which he wears to summerschool
and the teacher is afraid to lift it up.
Don't call Mama, we all beg,
Mama has a pirate headache.
Baby Jane has whooping cough.
Our father's in Korea dropping bombs,
says Lucifer.

I can draw and paint and rhyme:
Suckery puckery pudding and pie
Hope is a matador, ready to die
First of September remember to burst
Red is the color of Lucifer's lie.

JEAN-MARIE

I swear I didn't do anything
to make her call me names.
It's not my fault the boys all
follow me home.
I have to understand
I have to explain
how Mama loved the city, loved her books
her skyscrapers, museums--
now she hates the whole damn town
my Papa stuck her in.
No letters from Korea--
just bills and coupons,
letters from the principal.
If things keep up this way
our sister Jane won't ever
know her Papa.
Maybe I'm the only one who
saw his soldier side,
knew he was handsome and good
just knocked up by life.

Empty bottles in the kitchen
I am not the frigging maid.
Last night the baby's diaper
felt like 20 pounds.
I changed the crib and sang the
Tender Shepherds song and
over my shoulder Mama's tired
eyes, apologies and hugs
trying to erase those
things she shouted out
in front of all the kids,
face all red and screamy
like an old fishwife,
wrinkled skirt like an old bed,
unmade.
Mama is lonely, I explain to Hope
who doesn't want to hear
just writes in that old notebook,
growing thinner every day.
Oh, Mama, see these things,
I try to say
but when she put her face to mine
her tears tasted like whiskey.

MUZZLED

The day Luke turned into Lucifer
my Uncle John brought Heinekens.
When the mosquitos got thick
we went up to the roof-loft
with the Patty Playpal Uncle John had brought.
First we traded clothes,
the doll and I,
then Luke cut off her hair
with pinking shears
and showed me how it melted
in the candle-flame.
A luna moth was tickling my nose--
the candle smelled like beer
and Luke put out the flame with fingers
wet with spit
then turned the mothwings into
powder. This is for a spell, he said.
Don't make a sound or witches
will steal both your eyes
and cut your tongue.
My Uncle's hand was covering my mouth
and Luke said it was just a joke.

Our next-door neighbor's front door
says *Beware of Dog*. His pit-bull
wears a mouth-guard even though
we know he doesn't have a mean-dog bone
and wags like mad at trick or treaters.
No chance not to bite,
a muzzled dog is not going to lick your hand either.
At best he can sneeze for you.
Biters can be kind, too.
After all you can't really blame him for
wondering what you had in your closed fist.
Curiosity is not by nature vicious
although cat-killing can be
satisfying.
Ask Lucifer.

PAPA

My father was handsome,
or so my Mama says,
especially in the uniform
he wore to Korea.
I remember laughing,
my Mama's hair waved and shiny
for the camera.

My father is a memory
not a man, and I know about
memories—if you use them
too much they turn into lies.

My father,
I recall,
was kind to strangers.
When the front door opened
a fresh sunrise lit
the newspaper face
he wore like a bathrobe fit
to cover pride or shame

but when they'd gone,
sitting in his chair
declared Jean Marie's suitors
unsuitable,
assessed
with one eye on the door,
'You and your sister together
have less than half a brain.'

I never called him Papa.
I never called him.

MAMA

One man's ceiling
is another man's feeling;
your trash, his stash
not merely unwanted
but haunted and hunted
beneath old floorboards
where one man's ghost can be another's
guest.

One man's feeling is another man's
stealing
especially among thieves who
only find what they are looking for
somewhere else

and of course we learn from the saints
one man's kneeling
is another man's healing
although there is absolutely nothing I can do
about this sickness, here,
because we know
one man's kissing
is another man's missing.

One man's traveling
is another man's unraveling;
the leaving, the grieving;
the staying, the slaying.

Perhaps more than any other you know
how I could go on with this
ad infinitum,
all the way home
where one man's wife
will stupidly rhyme herself
with life
or knife
for the sole benefit
of someone who has already
become another.

BLACK WATER

The first stop
on the way to the Connecticut River
is for bologna-and-Hellman's-on-white
in waxed paper
that crinkles like magazine pages.
Even the idea of mayonnaise
is impossible. Crust is indigestible
and smells like dogshead
but compromise
and uniformity are the theme
on family trips where surveys might show
that no one gets their way.

The second stop
is cousin Laney throwing up,
the small yellow pleasure
of disembarking in the vague fog
of Dramamine which slows
the onset of hunger
pains when you are seven or ten,
or fifteen and growing.
There is usually a clinical opportunity
to examine the stringy pink and white bits
clinging to green-green grass
which seems unruffled by frantic flies
who somehow sense a party.

This year a small-town carnival with rides
became a spontaneous digression
after adult discussion.
Children with strange accents
working booths
seemed sad and old and free.
One who couldn't have been
more than twelve offered me a Winston.
I summerdreamed of this boy
so many times along with eely things
which kept my feet from touching
uncharted bottoms
of our designated slice of riverbed.
We gorged on carnival cotton candy
and the Mad Pirate Swing

insured that Laney was no longer
the sole vomiter.

Our arrival is unheralded and grouchy,
with always something missing
from the house which once was grand
but now is bent and soggy.
Besides bathing and fishing
there are the walks
in Nature Study Woods
where trees are labeled and signposts show
prime spots to dig for arrowheads
which seems impossible.
Lucifer complained that they were fakes,
that no Indians
had ever set foot in Connecticut
and although he was punished
I believed him. I could never distinguish
between a man-honed ancient
weapon of stone
and a vaguely three-cornered
geomorphic discovery
which seemed a genuine miracle.

We kept our findings
in a wilted PF Flyers box
in the ground-floor dressing-room of cement
which smells of damp
and sewage and bleach.
A rusted ancient showerhead offers
COLD only and faded oilcloth
stripes conceal the Dames' and Gents'.
We have to double up for time;
I am partnered with my Aunt
who wears lipstick and matched fingernails
even in the morning
and breakfasts on cigarettes and coffee,
whose darkish curly triangle in the Dames'
seems always at eye level.
Dirty blonde, my Mom says,
although struggling close-up
with my suitstraps
I can squint her into Marilynity.
Park Avenue was their birthplace,
where girls are tall
and smell of spice

and better things to come.
Later she will leave my handsome uncle,
or he her, for an Italian.

I might one day leave
my highschool boyfriend DC,
or he me,
at a neighborhood Italian restaurant
where the mineral-water
tastes of our undesirable
but safely roped-off pen of river.
I swallowed enough summer mouthfuls
to recognize that the going is usually better
than the destination anyway.
Mama says when I grow up
and leave this godforsaken place
called home,
from a plane I will see the Connecticut River
as the black snake she always suspected.

KISS

My first kiss was a palindrome.
His tongue was exactly
the same temperature as mine
although nothing else matched.

The wetness was nauseating
and the August beach-river air
anti-breathtaking
but I tried not to care.

I vomited all night,
most likely from the clams,
but I wasn't sure,
and couldn't tell my mother.

So I concentrated
on the line between sea and sky
even though it was nowhere

until the tides of my stomach
began to ebb
into nautical dreams of love
and heartwreck.

Later that summer I learned
a boyfriend is someone
who can touch you anywhere
and you don't stop them

even when you don't touch yourself,
who tells you it's been years
since bombs were dropped
anywhere near Korea.

WAY WAY DOWN

In school I play bass fiddle
because I have strong fingers.
You use a bow
which feels more like an arrow.
In music class we learned about
the history of Jazz
and listened to the bass parts
thumping like a heart.
I rested the bow and plucked along
with my right hand
and something happened.

So on the way home I stopped at the library
to see how they looked, these musicians,
to see if there were any girls--
and there was one—on bass like me.
Fourteen days with a photograph
even though I'm not allowed
to take the bass home
I can practice keeping my eyes half-shut,
lips slightly open, left eyebrow roofed.

Before I go to sleep I imagine running
down the streets of New Orleans,
fifty years ago,
everything all grillwork and sepia
and hearing Buddy Bolden's cornet
calling at you like a siren—
before there were cars,
before there were police bellowing
through the parting crowds.
Faces the color of caramel and toffee glistening
teeth sparkling through lips parted
for singing
in the key of way way down
cannot slow these emergency feet.

A siren calling you to arms...
or something like sex...or sax—
you forget now--
the grillwork curlicues
like a musical score you run down

with the breath and the pumping
and your dress clinging like a suit.

And he the jazzy cornet descant
beckons you to somewhere under
where it is cool and unlit and sweaty
and my heart pounding
with café au lait fear
and the rhythm of the bass.

JEAN-MARIE'S SEPTEMBER *WHEN I WAS A GIRL*
COMPOSITION WHICH I WROTE FOR 2 PINK MOTHER-
OF-PEARL BARRETTES (SHE GOT A- MINUS)

When I was a girl my favorite show was American Bandstand.
Actually it was my mother's favorite
and I watched it to feel older,
assuming it was sort of a big-girl version
of Winky Dink or Ding Dong School
to teach the ABCs.
American Bandstand, Dick Clark--
Chuck Berry Bo Diddley
Bobby Darin Chubby Checker--
I was excited to find everyone
who was anyone
occurring at the beginning of the alphabet
as opposed to the newspaper
headline people
who looked boring anyway
although they, too, appeared
exclusively in black and white.

Buddy and the Crickets, Della and Del,
Dion, Diana and the Connies...
sang with music that I liked to think about
under the covers at night...
voices breaking and yodeling,
girls sometimes producing a tear
in their carefully black-rimmed eye
when the camera came in for a closeup.
I could almost spell their names
or at least the first part,
these being the letters I had mastered
with DOG and CAT and BALL and APPLE
in happy colors on my lunchbox.

And then like my morning shows
there was the inevitable boring number part:
The Contest.
But even this was bearable
because of the dancers
who made Cubby and Annette
with the silly ear-hats
seem like cartoons.

And the way they moved
and interacted,
each with their own well-practiced
style, like matched dolls
with real makeup and hair
doing anti-gravity things
our barrettes could never accomplish
no matter how hard I shook my head
in the mirror.
Some were regulars—
I looked forward to their change of wardrobe
every week: an occasional haircut, new earrings.
I studied everything about them,
checked our kitchen chart every day
for signs of growth, cursing
my pathetic preschool roundness
in the mirror.

Then one day an unknown letter
from the planet of love and sex: Fabian.
No matter how close I sat, it wasn't enough.
I renamed my best teddy,
promised my cousin
a whole year's allowance
to trade me a button.
In our small-town world
no one had a name like this.
Fabulous, fire engine, fanbelt, french fries, Philadelphia..
all these now had a tiny thrill.
I envied my best friend Francie her initials.
And although they played his song
for weeks,
he never came back.

When Lucifer was punished for smoking
we all lost television access
and consequently learned about missing—
even the kind that could be blinked
on and off by a cruel parental hand--
and the enormous lasting value of things
that were that great word *obsolescent*,
because now that we have 20 channels
and can dance,
Fabian is nowhere to be found.

LANDMARK

The day DC carried my books from History,
in those days it was World not Global
I am quite sure
because from kindergarten on
I knew this was the sound our town made
as it whirled around the sun
while we slept and I dreamed
of stars and cities swirling
the way we twirled ourselves
when we were bored
into space-girls
pinned by gravity to carpets
watching the sky-molding above
orbit the room.

So on this day
the stringstraps of my wholeslip
causing shivers underneath
my school-jumper as I walked home
yes hugging I realized
this small pyramid of looseleaf binder
and books I needed
to squeeze the quivering back in.
The horse chestnut tree
my first-ever landmark,
the sign for bearing left
where the road split into School or Woods.
My tree held up a sort of arm
and waved me on twice every day--
braids or ponytail or pageboy or
new bangs like the Hullaballoo girls.

And this day of new landmarks
I found hard to keep inside and
even DC was all twitchy
when he handed me the books
and touched my arm, just here
where it felt different and zingy now.
So instead of bearing
I yielded
to the silliness of squeezing my old tree
which felt bumpy

and cooler than I expected.
And I hear this motor sound creeping up
then idling I think is the word,
with the malfunctioning muffler noise
like a car clearing its throat
but hovering while I pretended
I was measuring the tree for Science
and heard the car radio
crescendo as the window rolled down--
with a small jerk at the end of each crank.
And sideways I can see
the teal blue tailpiece,
backwheels raised up of a 1960 Chevrolet
I knew well from catalogues.
And I am thinking Wow, a junior-boy
congratulating me
on our freshman concert Monday
where I strongly debuted on bass violin.
His head comes out slow like a turtle
and I turn and he is leaning
all the way out now
and tilts his neck just right
so his long hair falls
perfectly off his forehead—
cascades, I think, as he says both my names
with no accents like he is reading
from a list-- and then he says it,
this thing that branded:
"I want to be inside you"
looking right into me
so at first I thought
he wants to feel this,
my tornado heart…
but in the extra second
the look brought this shockwave
like a frayed toaster cord
and I ran the 800-Meter home
thinking about my perfect even
quarter notes
thumping and pumping all the way
up the eight steps
down the flagstone path
into my bedroom
where all day
I had looked forward
to playing and replaying

that walk with DC down B-Wing Hall--
our first public walk--
and touching my arm just that way.

But instead this lizardy
creeping down toward my legs
and waves of slithery heat
which melted but didn't die down
as I expected, all night,
and grew worse at breakfast
where with horse-chestnut shame
and no appetite
I quietly pondered a new road.

CLASS TRIP

I remember
on the sixth grade bus
to the Natural History Museum
Ricky A. put his head in my lap
on the long ride home.
It was kind of like a deer head,
the way it felt heavier
than I would have imagined.
He slept and I resisted
the temptation of petting his soft hair
like an animal, like a mother.
My mother never does this
even though I wish she would.

After a long time, my leg was falling asleep
then totally numb, and he woke up.
And I put my head in his lap
and he didn't stroke my hair
but after a while I felt a hard lump
in his pants, and I didn't pick my head up.
And then I heard this very soft moaning
against the bus-motor noise
and the singing from the back—
the Ninety-nine Bottles of Beer on the Wall song--
and the hardness rising
and he pressing my head
softly, with his hand. And I knew
it had something to do with me
but also nothing about me.
Still, I felt a certain power,
and a little bit of shame.
I never spoke to him;
he's not one of my crowd.
But next trip— the nuclear power plant--
he asked to sit with me.

That night my Mom was on her bed watching TV.
I was trying to find a way to lie down
next to her—to put my head in her lap--
to feel her stroking my hair.
But it didn't work out.

EYE OF THE CAMEL

Tillary's cat has a fever
and we are praying to an Egyptian
goddess that she recovers and has more
kittens even though Tillary's father
had to drown the last litter.
She didn't seem to care much,
not like Mama when she lost our baby girl.
Since then she hasn't quite been right,
Jean-Marie says, despite the birth of
healthy Jane whose laugh is what she calls
infectious but whose diapers
are a filthy pain.

Dead babies are in a special room of heaven
filled with kittens, bears and colored sky.
We never got to see our baby sister;
straight to heaven she was whisked
by angels, Jean-Marie said,
in an instant, while
our Mama stayed in bed for weeks
and no one came except the doctor
with a hypodermic
and I learned the difference between pins and needles
is the eye.

Needles, things that prick,
one crucial s from without
need for such things
through which I thought
one could occasionally
glimpse the kingdom of God,
also remind of the breath of a camel,
something I experienced by accident
dismounting, improperly,
from my zoo-ride
setting off not just an exotic braying,
but a whiff of the man who sells hotdogs
and pinches, with the cigarette in his teeth
and the desert lips
and the camel grin
which I prayed will keep him
from fitting through
any old door.

JEAN-MARIE: TODAY THE BOY

Today the boy
on the Health Clinic elevator
which smells like piss and worse
stalled between seven and eight
shifts from left to right
and back, feels for his cigarettes,
nearly meets your eye,
reading graffiti about being
stuck in an elevator,
bleeding soundtrack from his transistor earpiece,
forearm tattoos blurry and cheap,
asks the time, like it matters.
Shit, he mutters, and then
leans down to you
where you can smell his inside,
everything he is in a sigh
which you do not answer just breathe,
because there is only your mouth as
his arm makes a bridge
over you pinned to the wall
unwilling to show fear.
His kisses
are soft and clicky and deep
and opening,
his scent is down your throat,
one boot steps closer so you can
feel his tall thinness,
his hardness growing against you
belt to belt; you must fight the need
to touch him *there*, but three-finger his face
softly, and he likes it. Now you are kissing
his ear and he is sort of purring
and you are remembering things that will
hurt if you miss them.
You have the premonition
of cheap stale beer and gritty wood
floors, a leather jacket on the chair,
dirty morning-after air and cigarettes
on the fire escape,
the endless entertainment of traffic
with that first black coffee,
music-- rock and roll

from the Hi-Fi inside--
smoking with the gargoyles
in dirty tenement heaven
you are filled up.

The boy in the elevator
who is skillfully undoing his heavy belt
with the one free arm,
says something in your thirsty ear
which you cannot quite get.
Things he will give you:
Cupid with a bullet now,
a song that says things like
'This ain't gonna be no playground romance".

And the elevator will not stall forever;
eventually you must come down,
eat. His eyes will narrow slightly
as you step onto the sidewalk,
show the desire you couldn't see
when he was pressed against you,
and you will stall for an instant,
maybe return his look,
say nothing and walk
as quickly as one can
with that heaviness
between your legs
which you will carefully
souvenir
like a glassblower's breath.

SCHOOL PHOTOS

Autumn is the longest season
especially when you try to count nights.
Jean-Marie says it is actually Spring
or Summer which have two months of 31.
My sister is smart, even though
my grades are better, most times.
Summer is like a slide
down smoothgrass hills--
it just can't ever be long enough.
Only DC makes these schooldays
bearable and collecting notes for observation
sheets. I do mimeo on lab Fridays
and take the extras home where I record
every detail I have seen
like an experiment.
Today he had a haircut which made his
Adam's apple look just a tiny bit
protruding. His collar was buttoned
but his neck looked maybe 4 millimeters fatter.
I know every shirt and all 3 pairs of Wranglers
like a brother. Also the black hightops
he wears on Wednesday gymdays.

The day of yearbook photos
he had a paisley tie,
a blue jacket that looked Mod,
Jean-Marie said.
The day he carried my books
I had on a dark green jumper--
the one I copied
from a Sears catalogue with a sky blue
blouse and matching barrettes.
I wore exactly this for yearbook photos
but was in the back
and only the barrettes showed.
DC smiled his crooked smile and now
we are forever on the same page.

I have figured out how to draw paisley:
first you make balloons
that melt and curve and then you put
scallops and designs around them, like lace,

then dot and color them.
My history notes are covered with these;
Tillary loves to turn the pages.
One day I'll show her how I camouflage initials in the swirls
but I can't trust her with this yet. Only Jean-Marie.

What will happen to the children in the picture,
Mama says with narrowed eyes after dinner
and doesn't use a question mark.
Some will be doctors, lawyers.
Some will lose their lives and legs in a war.
And some will be married to each other, I say
… at least one or two.
Doubtful, Mama says.
It is Autumn which is Fall and she
always counts years
by school terms or my birthday
which reminds her of how long
Papa has been gone.
I was born in Autumn and named Hope,
says Jean-Marie.
Rhymes with dope, says Lucifer.

DISECTION

You had to cut the line.
You don't have to press.
The scalpel will move with ease, she said.

How can a girl fear blood?
There is none they are fucking DEAD.
Embalmed, man, says my lab partner.
Then peel back.

But there is this tiny hole and if
you put the tip in, the body jerks,
I jerk, Ricky A. is laughing,
pretends to chew,
says Check out my Kermit-breath,
I feel my lunch coming, feel dry
baby-frog skin like earlobe,
dognose under my pinky
This little piggy-went-a-courtin'
Beat my scalpel
into pruning hooks.

No I say. *DO it* she says
NO takes firm my hand in hers,
fetal-soft skin slice
NO comes in a scream. *STOP IT*
The slap is sobbing hard, Ricky A. stops.
I will *NOT.*

At home in the bathroom
You don't have to press
Like a ouija finds blood comfort.

JEAN MARIE AND THE POET

A poet came to read at school;
he is renting a summer-cottage
somewhere in the mountains
even though it is cold
but that's how poets are, you see.
He is not quite handsome
but his hands move like dancers
when he speaks
and Jean-Marie thinks he is sexy.
His eyes are two parts white and three parts
cornflower— his mother must have
heard about the seeds.

Seniors-only get to have him in their
private English class
and Jean Marie is now going to babysit--
be his *Au Pere* which she wrote out O Pair--
his 2 lucky toddlers who will maybe grow up
to marry our Jane so we will be related.
His wife, says Jean, has waist-length hair
and paints. She wants to bring him
some of my notebook sheets but suddenly
I feel ashamed of all the paisley.

After his performance the Stage Band played for him.
I wore my dark green jumper and
when the musicians packed up, inside
my bass-case found a note that said
'Your eyelashes are a narcotic.'

Last June I inherited sunglasses
from my aunt but had to trim my lashes
so they wouldn't bump.
Mama noticed right away when she
came to tuck us in,
said like teeth these won't come back
and docked me my allowance
for all July, although
the punishment of short eyelash-bangs for life
seemed more than enough.
Well, they must have grown back.

Not that you look any less weird,
laughs Lucifer, and bets
One: something is going
on between Jean-Marie and the poet,
and Two: Mama won't give a refund.

AT NIGHT I DREAM OF ANTARCTICA

At night I dream of Antarctica.
Jean-Marie says it is the blue and white,
that everything I pick these days
is the color of snow and sky.
And even though the loneliness of it
terrifies me, there are penguins
to make you laugh,
and some belief I have always had
that bad things do not happen in the cold.
Or if they do, they are erased
by the forgiving snow,
the whiteness.

In art class we had to draw our faces.
Everybody had to pick a shape—oval,
square, round...mine was heart-shaped
which pissed me off, because I feel like
everyone can read my thoughts.
So just because my face is shaped like a heart
doesn't mean I have one, I said,
and didn't look at DC.
I drew my dark hair but I lied with the eyes
and made them the icy blue of the poet--
Antarctic blue.
I drew a sky-colored barrette in the hair.
The thing with pastels is, you can cover
dark with light, you can highlight.
Our teacher put mine up in front.

We had to write some words, a caption
for underneath our pictures. I kept thinking,
I already love you,
You touch me; I touch you
Even when you are sitting over there
By the bookcase,
Even though I have decided not to--
Touch you, that is.
But in the end I put
'At night I dream about Penguins.'

HOPE'S FALL POEM: THE LEAVING

My name is Meg or Lily.
Last night the leaving
was pages
ripping one by one
faster and faster
from a book I thought was mine
from a time when these were
still called leaves.

Is it still mine
even though it changed?
You rarely notice leaves
when they are still a tree
until they fall,
leave,
float softly like brown sailboats
catching Autumn breath,
ride up and back,
ring round the rosy
in whirls and twirls
they have practiced all summer
for a long last dance with the wind.
One, two, three, jump and fly
free and dizzy
but always down and down, they
crunch dead beneath your feet
or stay pressed forever
between the pages of your leaving.

Yesterday was a sad guitar
behind a door
that didn't open
and my name was
Emma Lee.

BLIND: FOR MAMA

Here is the film you do not watch:
in pale shades of grey dawn
a girl writes a letter.
Striped blind-shadows cross
her kitchen table.
Cigarette, black coffee, white cup
smoke curling into cream lace
curtains slow-dance,
loosened hair-strands,
window half-open to let
her silhouette,
her curved stillness
touch pale morning.

Now a café:
she slips the letter from her pocket
to yours. Open it. Read it.
This is important.
These things are important to her.
Very softly, the soundtrack--
but you are watching, waiting
for instructions;
Maybe she is singing for you.
Criss-cross,
the song and the shadows.
You are not listening.
You think because you need to touch her
it is okay,
this is a kind of love.
She writes every day—
a new letter—
maybe the same letter.
You do not find them
until she has gone.

In another window
a blind man
is looking for a box of letters,
feeling underneath the bed.
He hears her soft footsteps
crossing the street below
as she leaves the café.

He is weeping.
He is waiting for someone
who has given up.

You reach into your pocket:
find the letter,
all of the letters.
Now you are listening,
watching. Another girl,
a new shadow.
Criss-cross the table
where still she is gone.

Some days are like this—
betrayal after betrayal.
Sometimes it is faith,
sometimes just listening.
You learn to take your coffee black,
toast the weather.

LIFE GOES ON THE WAY IT DOES

Tillary says I am obsessed
not with poetry
but the poet.
Such a lovely word--
Obsessed...
It makes me feel grown-up,
gives me a purpose,
a consummate preoccupation,
perhaps even a psychosis
which would be a blessing
in the boredom of this old town.

Today we shopped for beads on Main Street.
You buy them in these
tiny plastic tubes
like chemistry experiments,
thread them onto fishing line
with a triple-fine needle.
Sea-Blue for a poet's eyes,
pink for my heart,
cobalt for Hope, white for the future.
Opalescent for obsession, I don't say.
We strung bracelets all day
and listened to the radio
in Tillary's basement.
Her Mom made sugar cookies with
colored sprinkles to go with our jewelry.
We looked at a magazine with pictures
of President Kennedy, his little girl
and his dark wife.
Sometimes the dark girl wins.

In Boston sprinkles are *jimmies*,
Tillary's Mom says.
In England they are *hundreds and thousands*.
I want to go to England—
find the house of William Blake
and Coleridge, Keats and Byron,
see what helped them find their words,
look through windows they looked out of at night,
watch the moon from that side of the ocean,
listen to the sea,

dream the dream of America
when it was still a baby like Jane--
soft and breezy, before it even had a flag.

I don't say these things, but I hate the US colors.
I don't mind so much white stars on blue,
but the stripes just look dumb as a barber's pole.
If I were Betsy Ross
I'd have done it green
with blue rivers and triangle mountains.
Maybe a horse, chasing the stars.
Maybe I'll paint a picture of my flag
and give it to the poet.
Oh God, would that be dumb.
So *juvenile*, as Jean says.
Best to keep your mouth shut,
like my sister knows how to do
when boys crowd around.
Like I do with DC. *Shhhh...*
he put his finger to his lips and then to mine yesterday,
like we have some secret shared obsession.

Tillary's Mom bought The End of The World
by Skeeter Davis
and it makes us nearly cry.
We played it sixteen times
for our age plus one for luck.
It's great except the part where she speaks
the words sound dumb after a while.
But it doesn't spoil it.
I wish I could play the song for Jean Marie
while we lie on her bed in the dark
looking out over the yard
with matching bracelets.
Hundreds and Thousands,
we say over and over,
like a spell.
The Pleiades are blinking...
Winken, Blinken and Nod, Jean hums.
I wish for four more sisters.
Hundreds and Thousands.

MAMA'S DEDUCTION

I didn't have a chance to teach you
about façade,
you being pure concept,
perhaps already a soul,
barely a thin blue line
in my poor Hope's notebook,
heartbeat of a cricket.

Was it my exhausted sighs,
housewifery complaints
and faked distress,
protests of motherhood clichés
that changed your unspoiled mind?
Maybe your tiny unformed eyes
could already see,
unborn Cassandra,
the smalltown world
that was your fate,
the piles of laundry,
crusted dishes in the sink,
the empty chair at meals,
the stink of loneliness
no pail of disinfectant can mask.

At a prescribed time
it is not convention
to have given you a name.
Only the Pope
might have called you someone.

I am not supposed to count you among
my losses,
children,
unhatched chickens,
tragedies,
official deductions,
although not a day has passed
when I did not miss the sorrows
in your unborn face.

ARTHUR MILLER I

Today someone was saying
or some song was singing
All of my Reasons
which were not reasons at all
but sacks of things
or valises that then reminded me
of Arthur Miller, whose play we read
in English class.
Even his initials seem perfect.
I want to write for him, to meet him
but what I really want
is for him to write *me*.

Outside the YMCA last week
a white-haired man—maybe a famous writer—
was picking up his granddaughter
from swimming class.
He was so happy to see her.
A great writer – and he was concerned
about her wet hair, whether she had eaten.
For her it was easy; he al*ready* loved her.
He was overjoyed to see her.
Even though he had the complex brain
of Arthur Miller and had been cruel
to his students about their writing
maybe even that day,
he was thinking about hot chocolate
and how to please this unpretty girl
with budding acne and pool-noodle hair.

I am sick of trying to make people love me,
of writing something
just so some Arthur Miller would pick me up
from swimming
or just want to,
or even pick up a telephone;
I wanted him to *already* love me.
So maybe this is the poem where I begin to be honest.
All the other ones are crap,
are trying to make Arthur Miller
or someone love me.
Except the '*l*' should be soft, somehow,
which seems impossible.

LUCIFER'S BAD MOUTH

Mama has a migraine
and I must keep the bubbly Jane
entertained.
I tried to teach her drawing on the Potsy step
but she was much more interested
in eating chalk.

Tomorrow it will rain;
it always follows headaches
and the days grow longer
without Jean-Marie.
She writes that she is getting smarter
every day,
reads Blake and Coleridge
and e. e. cummings
which at first I thought was a typo
but I know better now.

The poet is going on a journey
called Sabbatical;
we have to find my sister's birth-certificate
in case she needs a passport.
This makes Mama's headaches worse.
At least we had a Papa, Lucifer says,
and points to Jane
who does seem just a whit too giggly
to be part of our clan.

After supper he shows me
how he gets a buzz from Reddi-whip.
I'll bet that horny poet-guy
gives Jeannie something better,
says Lucifer, while Jane cries 'More!'
and holds her rosy tongue out
for another sweet white puff of cream.
Little bastard sister, he sings,
as he sprays, and 'You ain't my mother'
he snaps back when I cover
his bad mouth. Tell me something funny,
I beg him; *Please*.
At least the table-huffing

makes him laugh.
It's lonely here without Mama and Jean-Marie,
I confess to Lucifer,
who threatens if he has to eat my cooking
one more time
he'll commit *stewicide*.

COLERIDGE

Today our poet came to school
to do a workshop.
He brought me a barrette from Jean-Marie
who bought it with her salary
which when we were girls
we thought was a green leafy thing
you got from working.
Have fun with Coleridge today, she signed,
and don't write anything too good,
which made me squirm.
'Well, well, the dark-lashed writer Hope,
Your sister is a golden mermaid,' the poet said to me,
and showed a photo of her laughing, hair loose
and swingy like the magazine-girls,
throwing leaves
with his two babies.
Maybe Lucifer is right.

I know it is evil to be jealous of your sister,
but I am. Tillary says he gives her creeps
and Elizabeth Ann swore that he pinched her arm
and smells of whiskey.
But when he reads, the syllables hover in the room
and pictures like a soundtrack float
inside my head.
Even our teacher bats her eyes.
'I pity his wife,' says Tillary.
'Your sister's working
for a flirt.'
I am confused and mad
and sad and envious.
He wants to drive me home,
retrieve my sister's papers for the trip;
I cannot sit beside him in his car,
or let him up the eight steps;
even the flagstone path
is strewn with litter
and the house smells like a diaper.
So I lie and say I have orchestra practice,
become *complicitous*, a word we learned in World
rhymes with *solicitous*, which I am as well.
My sister has adopted a new family—

with father, mother,
brother, sister—other.
Oh why can't things be
as they were: messed up, depressed
and poorly dressed
but girl-clingy and free.
I don't want a mermaid sister,
I want to go to Europe
as a poet-wife, or stowaway
with Jean in a steamship hold.
It's worry that makes you old,
says Mama, frowning.
Sorry makes you scold, cold, bold, unfold,
I sing to set the smiles of Jane to giggling
baby laugh ribbons
which ripple through the kitchen
and wash us over
like waves of gold.

WATCHING FIREWORKS WITH JOHNNY AND DC

In dreams you're never naked
or alone but serious
and eyeful
weeping willow-spider legs of gold-ness
touching barely
asphalt rooftops down,
your hand around my half-consumed Corona
like junior prom, the truth,
some silly questions.

Why would anyone celebrate
July? And don't you much prefer
explosions from a block of ice?
In Mexico these rockets cost 10 pesos;
a warm cerveza on the bar
quizas por nada.

This must be your city, Johnny says,
a cigarette slow-burning
on the ledge
waiting for the barges to unhinge their cargo
beneath a dress so dark it could be cut from night sky
(Johnny once again).

Rarely have I seen anything so clear
as the edges of that island
chiseled out of moonless fireworks
except my future name
in sparkler neon like a crown
which melts
into black holiday afterburn,
a double on the house
and colder days ahead.

THE DRIVING-WITH-LUCIFER SONG

I'm driving, I'm not driving
Singing a cowboy song
Headlights shining on your face
And darkness in your eyes

Nothing in my rear-view
But a taxi ride to hell
Windows open and the cool oh-wind
Of city-dreams rushing into

All-night small-town summer sunrise
Every turn a movie opens, closes
Whispers, doesn't whisper things
Ears, mouth meet eyes, skin, skies

Every turn the warm-trash smell
Of each block thing familiar
So unwholesome
If I were blind I'd see it

Nights like these they say
Keep you in business
Nights like these remind of things
That never happened

Move too slow to flash your
Rear-view mirror, close
Enough to graze your silver bullet
You won't see me in your past

Remember how to drive, swear to erase
To ease this only place
The darkness in your eyes
And headlights shining on your face

MAMA - CARDIOLOGY

A mirror changes everything.
Even blindness can be sweet
before the diagnosis,
makes you think: if you can smash it,
it will stay this way forever,
it will be real.

All I ever wanted: something more
than your name on my tongue
like an apple.
The sorrow of knowing
things that never happened in the past
are ringing like a bell,
the absence of you in my deaf future.

It was the day they took apart
Johnny's father's heart, and
I was thinking about Valentines
or you, seeing the hangman's noose in every rope
and 'All roads lead to black,' you said,
refusing to believe you are untied.

But go ahead, smash the moment,
as though one of these sharp instances
will hold that piece of your complexion
you could stand to look at,
let alone mine.

I have always craved deep scars,
the invisible become visible,
your bruise a kiss from the dark God
who, if you decide not to refuse,
will bless you
with no more of this,
no fear of sleep, betrayal,
like an old white dress,
some version of this love tucked
in someone else's
cardboard box.

Feel the black wind
close your cardiologist eyes
and let all roads…

CIAO

A writer on sabbatical—left behind
strident students,
pressure to publish;
took the bottles,
took up sculpture. Ha.
On a slab of stone
unpolished
chipped away an image of love
that closely resembled the babysitter,
drank enough to crawl into her bed without shame,
begged in the coercive tongue of poets. Ah.

On her 19th birthday
took her to a small town in Tuscany
where on the lumpy iron bed
of a penzione they had
espresso and biscotti twice,
Montepulciano and pancetta.
On the third morning
said he had to leave;
it had nothing to do with her;
it was him. Ha.

His grieving family flew Alitalia.
Alone on the prepaid balcony
the babysitter confided in a
boy from Murano who balanced a
hand-blown paperweight on her stomach
while he placed contagious organisma
inside her. Ah.

Spending final severance lire
at a café, scrawled upon the writer's
clean-lined pad: 'Local wine is cheap
and with a thumbnail you can
block the moon. Ah.'

By the time she came back,
Mama was too fargone to punish.
Mustn't trust a poet, Jean-Marie said.
Mustn't trust a man, Mama corrected.
Lust must rust dust, I do not say,

but am glad my sister is back
even though she will have scars.
She unpacked two books of Ferlinghetti,
and one by the poet himself, inscribed
'To my mermaid prom-queen:
Long may you rain'
I am going to learn to appreciate Ferlinghetti,
especially the one called Coney Island.
Maybe this is where the heartbreaker is hiding now,
riding the Ferris Wheel in black and white,
searching for mermaids in the city.
I hear her crying when I awake at 4 AM.
I try to listen, not to talk too much. I don't ask
but I hope she learned at least
how to pronounce Rilke.

DAM

Some nights we drive up to the Dam,
Lucifer's favorite place--
he liked to say the word,
back when things like that made Mama
roll her eyes. Days of innocence.

Last night DC and Jean and I drove up
and smoked a joint.
There it is, all that water
and no one guarding it, I say.
But why would anyone steal water?
D.C. laughs.
Jean Marie is exhaling, says nothing,
doesn't speak much these days,
looks more beautiful than ever—
the sadness.

Kind of beachy here, but all this concrete
with the dark forms lurking
like sandcastle ghosts in the dark.
I can't quite understand
why this terrifies me,
a kind of hell
or somewhere I end up in dreams,
somewhere that reminds me
of something I have never seen,
of something I am missing,
of some huge monstrous thing that took place
that someone has built over.
The landscape of fear.

Looking through the books of paintings
so many landscapes, but not mine.
Except this one—by Dali—the bleak
sandy desert,
with strange things melting
and soft—like a dream.
The Persistence of Memory, it is called.
Jean and I, we are in the far,
far background,
tucked invisibly into the horizon,
sitting on the steps of the Dam,
hoping for a future.
The Sisters of Undertow.

MAMA (SCARS)

Things heal, things ridge over;
but they leave a mark, for people like me.
The line of you incises my night again—
etches into my crawl-space,
dull grooves I once knew
how to sleep through.
Funny how in dreams one is unscarred,
the way the soldier-amputees all say
they walk and run.

When I was whole I dreamed
of scars, of deep wounds received
like love as I stood on a tenement
staircase
while a tall man on a lower step
so he can be face-to-face
puts quiet bullets into my stomach.
Pumps, I think they say
in crime novels.
I can smell his breath of gunpowder
and something very distinctly
between rosemary and cardamon--
which makes me think in a former life
I was a gunshot victim,
precursor to the hole I was born with
in this one,
a thing that no one sees.

So back to the dream,
the first dream of you
since I gave up.
You dropped a shirt on my bathroom floor—
a shirt I don't remember from your wardrobe,
the fabric some stripey other-memory.
And I walked into you,
with the shirt silky and falling.
And you were kind, still kind
like when we were strangers…
And I realize it is not the strangeness
but the kindness
I miss the most…

the kind of tenderness of maybe
that third night which goes away
forever like some old
shedding,
does not leave a scar
no matter how much you wanted one.

Even though love when it begins
is like smooth cool stone
which I am feeling beneath bare feet,
we seek out the uneroded thing
that used to be this stone
before it gave up.
My love was not ever
something you could walk on,
something you would want to put in a pocket,
but some secret edgy roughness,
a slashed pain underfoot,
a relative of scare without the extra vowel
which with something partly dead
makes sacred.

Today, after the dream, I miss
the sense of smoothness I wore through
with my trademark drive to probe
even when you were gone,
long after I stopped being torn.

There are the scars now;
and scars, although they have a strange
numbness on the surface,
are always changing,
have a hidden side that never heals.
Sometimes they welt,
sometimes pull down
unpredictably,
with nerves that speak a pain language
that is never quite familiar.

So I guess despite initial kindness
we both turned rough on the inside.
I should have known, etc...
but that didn't stop me.
Like a small prodding beat
it pursued,
until our bed had an undertow

and our faith edges
and angels angles
and love began to
fall out.
At the farewell party
wedding wineglasses no longer held something
dark and liquid and clinky
but smashed and crashed and gashed.

Dreams, like death, are scarless.
Even the nightmares,
the ripping flesh-eating ones--
take place before scars have begun.
Soon that will be all that is left of me:
a spectral fossil of marks
like footprints on air.

CONFESSIONS

Tonight Jean-Marie and I
in the Emerald City
shared Marlboros with Johnny B
and his brother.
Jane was on the Potsy step
learning how to throw
and jumping like a crazed rabbit.
Jane doesn't care about lines.
We put the carblanket over us
and the sadness of Jean
through the smoke, her pale eyes,
makes her more beautiful
but I don't say.

Johnny moves to the Step of Confession.
I am wondering if Jean will tell
about the Clinic but when her turn comes
she says 'I didn't love him.
Not for a second.'
I don't say that I did.
But I show my new scars.
Johnny B's brother wants to be a hero
and Johnny tells how he peed in their kitchen
and blamed it on the dog
because he hates his Mom.
Next round Jean says
'His poetry sucks, too.
Hope in her sleep is a way better poet,'
But later Jean says she has scars, like mine,
even though they don't show.
Johnny's brother says
he doesn't miss his father
even if it's a sin,
says he didn't cry or anything.
I tell about calling the army
that night we found our Mom
on the floor when I was 13.

Before we go inside
I pretend to be helping Jane
find more flat stones
and move down to the third step
and wish for the scars of Jean.

JEAN-MARIE'S POEM WE WROTE TOGETHER WHICH
TOOK ALL NIGHT : THE MERMAID DOES COLERIDGE

I awoke this morning with the scent of Coney Island
on your hair, trying to assess the distance between
souvenir and omen, imagining my choice
if I were you, which I am not,
unless this is another dream:
to go look at unlabelled exotic flowers
or stay home listening for the snap of mousetraps.
And how to describe the gardens without words
when you doubt my vocabulary.
Ah, I will think, you should have seen the *gloaming*,
thinking this means the path of misted summer
breezes over grassy hills.
And just because I know nothing of sailing ships,
of masts and sails—
galleys, planks, knots, leagues, and fish,
of Coney Island, I cannot touch your poetry.
I am in fact afraid of water…
even though wherever you walk on this wet planet,
you will eventually come to the sea…
We are 97 % water; how can one fear oneself?
A lady on the bus today warned not to sit,
she'd been exposed to scoliosis.
I am trying to decide whether this room now needs
more walls
or shall we just tear down the ones that are?

I know you will be leaving, it hovers
like a black balloon,
ghost of evaporated sweat in closet air, here.
I am thinking about shopping for a cross necklace,
remembering how we crawled those cobbled steps
on bloody knees only to find a lipstick stain
on the altarpiece. Was that irony? Anachronism?
I have forfeited the right to question.
That woman on the bus today seemed grounded,
her clothing more appropriate than mine…
I asked about the Cyclone—I believed her.
Even her hair knew its place.

A couple at the traffic-light outside now—
he reaches across the carseat

with some assumption, ten years of intimacy.
We don't have assumptions, do we?
Her hair is messy.. how does she deserve this?

While you sleep I am still safe...
only the balloon at the window
either bigger or closer, I have no more perspective.
Is that what growing old means, getting larger?
Why can't you stay with me? I promise not to speak.
Those people you write for---they have had enough
of sails and masts and bowsprits...
You don't need this nautic audience...
These people are making you ill----
they make you feel inferior. You are drinking
for them and they don't know what you mean;
they are no different.
Okay, I lied when I claimed to understand;
I just wanted you to keep on talking,
to reach across the seat at some red light.
I am afraid of the sea, afraid I will be forced to swim,
even though I do know how, I swear.
If you leave me I will die of scoliosis,
eclipse in a balloon, evaporate.

Coney Island on my things as I unpack
this broken desert heart uncarefully.
If you dig long and deep enough
there will be water. I believe this.

HOPE MINOR

Lucifer got arrested last night,
third time since summer,
since he came of age,
this one for DUI and possession
of a weapon
even though it's only
a knife he traded for
with Johnny B.
I hope they confiscate it--
it's the one he used
to slice the garter snakes in half
just to scare us girls away
from the Step of Blood
and five years later
it still smells like reptile-guts.

Mama is fed up and wants him to move out.
He can't seem to hold a job; now with
the new arrests the only place that hires
is Woolworth's
and he hates the people. He hates
the whole town, just like Mama,
but they can't agree on anything else.
She says he takes after our Papa and soon
he'll get drafted, too. Fuck that, says Lucifer,
who doesn't like rules.
Johnny says he's selling dope
downtown; he tells us he plays cards for money,
cause he always seems to have enough for gas
and Mama's whiskey so she doesn't like to ask.
He has a new way of talking, kind of Southern,
and lets the words out of the side of his mouth,
like a cigarette. He has a funny scent—
not just the smoke and drink—
a kind of vinegary thing.

Says he was looking for that teacher-man,
would show him what he thinks
of poetry and child molesters.
But Jean is an adult, and all he did was break her heart
a little. Anyway, the cottage is abandoned and one day he'll get
what's coming to him, Mama says. They all do.

Lucifer wants a drink and Mama pours.
One for Jean-Marie, too.
She's earned the right to sing the blues.
Heck, only two minors left in this house, now.
I hate the smell of whiskey, and I do like playing Chopin
Arco in the dark minor keys.
Jane is definitely major.

WICHITA LINEMAN

Lucifer has two more weeks in Juvenile
where he won't mind that I have borrowed
his Emerson AM/FM.
At night I tie my blankets to the window-latch
and have a tee-pee for music.
Sometimes I wake up and can't tell if it's late or early.
I get up and plug it in the kitchen outlet,
start the coffee, cream-of-wheat for Jane and Mama.
If I had dogs this is when we'd go for walks.
They'd watch me carefully while I put the kettle on,
they'd lie across my feet like slippers.

Lately it seems they are always playing
Wichita Lineman. I hear this song and miss things.
I miss the dogs I never had. I miss driving
with Lucifer.
I know that this is the song that will play in my head
when I am grown and look back on these
high-school days, the days of loving DC.
First time I heard it, I knew I'd always have
that sense of looking out some window--
of looking back, of driving, of the white line.
And I need you more than want you,
And I want you for all time.
Just the way he says it—Which-i-taw--
gives me that feeling,
like standing around after DC's football practice
when he is all sweaty and tired,
that feeling that is not quite happy
and not quite sad,
because it is not really yours.
But you know you will look back on this moment
and get the Wichita Lineman feeling,
like missing dogs.

WHAT YOU LOOK LIKE WHEN I THINK ABOUT YOU

To calm myself at night
I list things; sometimes only you
and loneliness;

Some nights letters
will not come;
a noun is more than company.

When I am tired at last
I wish for one word
which would mean: everything…

Instead there are
a million ways to say:
I'm sorry, nothing.

A shadow
can make me cry now…
Light, a closing door, lists—Do not

speak, you say, because
you are already inside me.
Like the Wichita Lineman

and beneath all things anyway
is always one more thing,
breaks surface,

the way blood comes through
from the slightest cut….
I am holding in the madness.

ALL IS NOT LOST

Hallelujah, justice has been served.
Lucifer has been released and
our sister has been chosen for a pageant.
They're going to provide the dress and shoes
and all she has to do is fix her hair,
show up and walk.
She is beginning to sing again
and hanging out in town and going to dances.
Mama says once you show your pride
everyone forgets.
A man came up in Nightingale's, left his card
and came to call, all proper. It's just a local thing
to find a state contestant for Miss Dairy America
because Jean-Marie is creamy pale
and has these lovely cow eyes
and the hint of new-grass scent
when she forgets her Shalimar.
Just a local thing but she'll be on the news
and wins a scholarship if she's chosen.
I'm glad for her but still
I feel like I've been fifteen forever
and my chest is flat as playground asphalt,
says Lucifer.
Baby Jane can't get the hang of potty training
which is annoying, although all in all she is the icing
not to mention the candles and the sugar roses
on the stale sheetcake of this family.

The ground is thawing, spring is finally in sight
and the circus is coming for a week. Oh Jane,
you can't imagine what you're going to see!
I'm going to find some library books and show her.
Jean will drive to town in Lucifer's car—
his license has been taken, but we'll
find DC at practice and roll the windows down
and play the radio so everyone can hear.
Please Mama, come with us... we'll get flowers
from the park and look in store windows.
But Mama lights a Winston and looks careful.
Pass, she says, exhaling perfect circles
in which Ringmaster Jane inserts her hands
like bracelets.

KIDNAPPED, FOR JEAN-MARIE

I must amputate this vintage heart
that you have had far too long,
put it in a cedar box
that I will kidnap,
tie up in the trunk
of an unlicensed black hearse
and drive through states
that have more syllables than this one—
and fewer letters.
I will muffle its deep breathing,
until the exhale is low and major key,
girl of the sea
who will have the earth.
I will take it out only
when he has escaped
and will be safely memory.

Through my hands on the wheel,
my feet flooring these old pedals,
enter the rough and smooth
that is America Accelerata...
all the way to baked Alaska
days and road-nights
windsocking from my head
like a highway Medusa singing:
Here I come, heart in mouth,
Heart in trunk,
Oh say can you sing,
The Untied Snakes
Of Harmonica
Ad hoc
Huius, huius, huius
Hunc hunc
Junk trunk.

BALLET SHOES

Lucifer's in trouble again.
Probation officer said no more strikes.
And then what, Mama asks?
He gets the chair for stealing railway flairs?
But this was unarmed robbery,
Breaking and Entering.
How can you take things without arms
I want to ask in his defense but don't.

'If you'll excuse me Ma'am,'
says Mr. Goldberg to our Mama,
'that boy of yours is suffering
from lack of a father.'
And how about these girls here,
Mr. Goldberg? Do they look like
suffering too?
In the car Mama looked like she was crying.
'Hope, I'm running out of time,' she said.
At least she didn't say
I'm running out of Hope.
And Lucifer's bail took all the money
we no longer have.

So it's not the day to ask for ballet slippers.
Tillary has pink and blue and white;
you sew on your own strap.
Anyway, I think I want blue ones, with the pink
sewn on, or pink with blue, I can't decide.

Jean-Marie cooked hamburger stew
while Mama napped with her drink glasses
like a chorus line on the night-table.
When we called her in to eat she said
'There was an old woman who lived in a shoe
with too many children and overcooked stew.'
Jean turned red and Lucifer said noone asked
to be born and if she did ask he would've refused.
Then no one spoke. I think it is unfair
that no one talks about the pageant.
Under THINGS I'VE NEVER DREAMED
I drew Hope running out of time
in Jean-Marie's new dress
with palest blue ballet shoes.

MISS DAIRY DIARY

The day of the pageant starts out raining
but clears. Tillary's Mom is picking us up
because ours is too ashamed to show her face
with Lucifer and all the trouble.
The Dairy girls have their own float
with a cow and milkmaids in costume.
Three tents on wheels with juggling clowns
and acrobats precede them,
then seven elephants wearing bells and satin ribbons,
marching all serious trunk-to-tail
except the young calf at the end
swinging his colossal baby head back and forth
like a puppet. Dancing in the key of Jane.
Our stage band is performing two pieces from
Carnival of the Animals even though
we are under-rehearsed. Jean looks
like a fairy princess
all in white except the crown of leaves.
'Don't get your hopes up,' Mama warned,
'these things are fixed,' but had to admit
our Jean looks like a true Queen.

As it turns out, she comes in third
which is a relief because Lucifer's bail
used up the travel fund for the finals.
She wins a US savings bond,
a Sears Roebuck catalogue certificate
and the prettiest moonstone necklace
in a silver box with sky-blue cotton
I would die for.
The band was not too shabby,
Mr. Goldberg said, and DC carried my bass
all the way from the schoolbus and back
and smiles at me during the 4-measure rest
before the coda. I feel good, and proud of my sister
who is signing more programs than the winner.
She also gets us ringside circus seats for Saturday
and extra cotton candy to take home to Jane,
with hotdogs and containers of chocolate milk.
We drive off like celebrities at sunset
waving streamers from the window.
Tillary's Mom says Jean wins

not only Most Ethereal
but Most Definitely Destined For Fame.
and joins us all singing with the car radio
Jean, Jean, the roses are red…
Come out of your half-dreamed dream.

BEADS

When we get back from the pageant
police cars are at our house.
Oh, no, Mama...
But Mama is in the kitchen
with all the uniforms.
Maybe our Dad, I think...
Jane is tugging at the holster
of the one with red hair.
All their hats are taken off.
From the doorway
Jean is screaming.
A sheet shaped like a human
on Lucifer's floor
and first aid things all around...
a kind of pump.
It smells like puke,
and always the stale whiskey.

After a while we find out
Lucifer jumped out
when they were taking him
back to Temporary Juvenile.
I guess he wanted to see Jean
in the milk-white dress. Oh Lucifer.
They chased him; he ran home
and took some stuff—along with
Mama's sleeping pills.
I don't know what to feel.
The minister comes by, says
to our Mom 'Your boy's been
running down this road for years,
now.' Can't they just say something
good? He's dead.
'My baby,' Mama's crying,
in a way that makes me hold my ears.
Hard to think of Lucifer
as anybody's baby.
Johnny B's mom forces me and Jane
to come over. Jean is an adult and
she can make her own mind up.
I need Jean. I keep thinking about
the boy and the leaking boat in the story.

How there are more holes
than fingers.
Johnny's Mom lends me her cross,
her beads. I'd rather have my own,
the ones I strung with Tillary
but I don't say.
All night she forces me.
I feel like throwing up and can't.
I need to cut. The beads, she says.
And shows me how to say Novenas.
I pretend I am a blind girl
learning how to count.
When dawn comes I sneak back.
I am thinking about school, about DC,
but Jean says death takes precedence.

In Lucifer's room the sheet is gone.
Jane is napping in Jean's bed, in the
pink rabbit pajamas with feet.
I scrunch up next to her, so warm
and Jean comes too, huddled like puppies
we are, my sisters and I.
Now I am crying, the kind with no sound.
I am wondering if blind people pull the curtain
in the morning, if they can feel the light.
I guess that's what the birds are for.
In my head I can hear Lucifer saying
Hope, Hope, Rhymes with Dope.
He looked so long under the sheet.
Long Tall Lucifer.

MAMA - BONES IN THE SAND

How to bury a child:
You can't.
We couldn't save him,
the doctor said.
Liar.

This one was hard to carry,
fought me from the get-go.
Felt like a baby giraffe inside.
When I got to the hospital
he had kicked bruises between my ribs.
Too big to fit through…
Stayed in there too long,
the doctor said.
I believed in doctors then.
Had to cut him out,
separate us.
Hadn't drawn first breath
and we were already wrestling.

You can't bury an elephant.
Too big. And the other elephants
won't let you. In the Sahara,
the body just lays there.
First the food chain, next
maybe some nesting material for birds,
then bones in the sand.

I haven't hugged my living son in so long.
When I came close it hurt
I could see quills go up.
It was painful to even talk,
to look at me.
At night I'd tiptoe in-- make sure
because his breathing was dead quiet.
I'd lay my head on the bony giraffe-knees,
listen-- smell the pillow.
When I changed his sheets
still kept my distance,
tried to respect boy-secrets.

An elephant remembers,

skin the color of dread.
That one mother, trumpeting
the same killing Miles note
from Porgy and Bess.
The herd, urging her.
But she can't.
She can't leave.

How to bury this child?
Other mothers have done this.
Maybe it is comforting
to spread yourself across damp ground,
rest your face on the cool headstone.
But what am I thinking?
He will wake up. He always wakes up.
He will open his eyes, tell me
Get the fuck out of my room.
The sweetest words I ever heard.
Come on.
Remember that time
he hit his head on the court?
Your heart stopped.
Actually stopped.
And he was faking.
Got up and laughed.
Didn't look at you.
Go! Go! The stands yelled.
I am on my feet.
My heart is stopping.
Wake up.

In the Sahara the mother elephant
is running her trunk
over the bones.
Scanning…making sure.
Remembering.
Softly snorting, not trumpeting
because the herd has moved on
and the predators will know
she is alone with her grief.
She can't leave.
Back and forth, she scans the bones,
shakes her huge head.
Sand in her eyes.
Bones in the sand.
You can't leave.

HOW TO DRESS

How to dress for a funeral:
because you can't think.
You can't remember.
But somehow you know, for all time
you'll remember your dress.
The shoes. Looking down.

The last thing I remember him saying
is 'Party of One', and me thinking
just because there are people
and there is a restaurant,
why does that make it a party?

They said good things about him
at the service. Afterward
my Uncle John said Luke was a boy
who could've used a war.
I remembered how he gave Matt Levitt
the scar, how he made Johnny B
give back our dead Barbie.
And how nobody drove faster.

Jean-Marie remembered
what a good pirate he was.
And how nobody drove faster.

Mama didn't say anything
and had a veil. She wore her
honeymoon shoes which looked
brand new.
Tillary loaned me pink ballet slippers
but they seemed all wrong.
Also there was mud at the cemetery
and walking up the hill.

The worst part was leaving him there,
because it started to rain
and you start to think Oh no, we've got
to bring him home, wrap him in blankets.
But the minister said this was just his shell,
that he was in our hearts now
and his soul in Heaven.

Let's hope so, he might have winked,
if it was someone else.
Still it felt all wrong. Forever.
Worse.

THANKSGIVING

Lord explain to me
how You brought me here--
what grace, thanksgiving
carried me into the where
of this the next-to-far-
too-many tired ceremonies,
platitudes and heads
in parallel rows at wide-planked pews
cut from wood of grandfathers
extended with a bloody
hammer and saw--
his portrait face
peering up from long-boiled soup
they dole afterwards.
You can cut the air with a spoon,
lift the breath of the sitting dead
to unparted lips.

But you,
you are spinning
not like a wheel
or gyro-- this would be normal--
but spinning with the tale they told you
was tall but is yours,
spun like sweet cotton of glass,
of things that could be sharp
and deadly if you swallow
but bind you like your own rope
to these people,
to something you might have been,
somewhere you might be drawn
because you cut and cut and
you don't want to call attention.
So you loosen like a stole
wrapped for warmth
even though the fibers stick at your neck.
And you are smiling,
sitting on your hands.

Be still your mother looks at you.
Be still your chin warns rope
of something you may not shed

tonight.
Old soup inflames your throat
though you refuse to swallow
and you close your eyes
as candlefires burn into your
black eye pain,
the same that signal
unblindness.

When you awake
in blankets of dread
the noose of morning
takes your breath away,
leads you by cold nose
to some planked place
where you in single file close in
on next-to-last grace.

MAMA - JUMPER

One does not make the leap upward,
not in this world,
as the first jumper found.
Praying perhaps for 'up', they leapt,
or for the endless fall.
It did not happen.
And love is a sorry foothold
when you feel the distance multiply below.
Even schoolchildren are taught
falling bodies gather the effect of mass;
but this is afterthought.
We choose to jump, not necessarily to smash;
when the abyss is open, love is just a drop.

That first girl jumper—maybe she used to dream
about standing on the ledge,
and then she would fly...
Love could have been that ledge, that sill—
a rope, a door, the bloody rags, a souvenir--
a tired meal, a tear
in the rotten bottomless bucket
of all the regrets she could think up
in these panicky minutes, and maybe
someone else's confession, because her own would be
pointless and boring,
would not provide the momentum she will need.

And you know, she may be thinking,
even if they find a few fingers and some doll bits,
they still like to put them in a man-sized coffin,
out of respect or maybe guilt
or embarrassment at the graphic horror
a compact box might inspire--
the image of a crushed cube made of human
meat parts. Vacuum packed.

Maybe she was able to fool herself,
to admit:
You are the room
from which I choose to perch myself
on the ledge of love
for nothing--

for the useless freefall one could disguise as a launch
if the building was on fire,
and you can't remember which one to pick,
Icarus or the one that sounds like death,
and blindly jump into that sun.

LETTERS UNDER THE PILLOW

We are spending a semester in New York
with our Park Avenue Aunt
we know so-so from Connecticut.
Mama thinks it a bad idea,
but she is going to a place
where they will make her better, too…
a cure for sadness.

Our minister swears we will be back
unless we change our minds.
We won't.
We can't leave our brother alone
on that hill, no matter what the
minister says about the soul.
And who will teach the girls
to skip the Seventh Step?
Lucifer was never superstitious
and look where it got him.
Johnny B says Lucifer was a kind
of hero. His brother seconds the motion.
Their Mom lets me keep the beads.

In the car my aunt lets us choose the radio.
No bologna sandwiches, she says.
I'll go to school with my cousin Laney.
And Jean—why, Jean could be a Cover Girl,
she says. She's going to make us all rich.
Jane stinks up the car. My aunt finds it
appalling that she's nearly 3 and still
in diapers. Like a wild animal, she says.
Jane shakes out her curly locks and
tries to say New York.

Our rooms have tall windows and the
city sky is grey.
Somewhere downtown my painting
waits: The Persistence of Memory.
Our Aunt has a Dalmatian which Jean says
has taken to me like a sister.
We call our Mom on Sundays.
DC writes me.
Actually writes.

He's getting private drum lessons.
The football team's in nearly last place,
The Stage Band misses my bass fiddle.
'Bad. We suck', he says. 'Miss you, DC.'
Life is like curtains.
Opening, closing.

ENDINGS

We are supposed to talk about closure.
That's what the minister said.
Closure is what happens in movies,
on TV. In real life there are questions--
the kind everybody asks and the kind
you can't bring yourself to ask.
Like my brother was a person, but
for so long there was nothing to say.

Some art—like those Salvador Dali paintings—
they are still open, too. And some poems.
We talk about them in school. They end
but they are still open. Except maybe
the sonnets of Shakespeare. The last
two lines—like matched French doors closing
on the poem, all nice. And you walk away
with a meaning. Maybe something secret inside,
like in a bedroom, but a meaning.
Not so my brother's death.

Still there is always a moment
when you know something is over—
or something is changed forever...
Like Jean said the way the poet looked at her
that last morning. She knew.
Not necessarily the last glimpse
of a car tail-light on a dusty road, receding--
that is so cinematic—the way I'd like to
imagine my brother, driving away.
Not even necessarily the first shovelful of dirt
hitting the top of the box
when they lowered him into the ground—
the same ground he smushed his face in
when he jumped off Johnny B.'s garage.
The foreshadowing, I am thinking,
because this is how they teach us
in Manhattan
to look at literature: stuff the author puts in
to foreshadow the great event.

My brother's life was no book.
But the ending thing—

for me it was coming home
after the funeral,
seeing his bed all made up and neat
like it never was—that's when I knew
he wasn't coming back.

And the Wichita Lineman
is still on the line.

FLOATERS

From the corners of eyes
and rooms
these ghosts have become
bold as mice
crossing tiles
at eyeblink speed.
I used to think this
paranoia
but I'm quicker now.

Things that float:
dead fish,
a missing dog,
iridescent noodles
in my cornea.

Things that don't:
shells,
tattoos,
despair.

I learned the dead man's float
in the black Connecticut River
with the guppies or minnows
(no one knew the difference)
in packs that tickled.
My legs would always sink
down to the disgusting
sliminess of the bottom
like a *girl-magnet*,
an expression my older brother used
along with others like
pussy and *slut* and *finger-fuck*
and later on *nod* and *wasted*.

One night he left to get cigarettes
and came back with a
magical mermaid tattoo
which was beautiful and smooth
and terrifying
and still winking

from the shoulder of his corpse
when he OD'd in his room.

Six feet under,
I like to think of her at night...
floating...